A Character Building Book™

Learning About Strength of Character from the Life of
Muhammad Ali

Michele Ingber Drohan

The Rosen Publishing Group's
PowerKids Press™
New York

For Laura and Doug—because you guys are "the greatest"
Special thanks to Nancy Ellwood, friend and editor extraordinaire

Published in 1999 by The Rosen Publishing Group, Inc.
29 East 21st Street, New York, NY 10010

First Edition

Book Design: Erin McKenna

Photo Credits: p. 4 © David P. Allen/Corbis-Bettmann; pp. 7, 8, 11, 15 © UPI/Corbis-Bettmann; p. 12 © Hulton-Deutsch Collection/Corbis-Bettmann; p. 16 © Archive Photos; p. 19 © Neil Rabinowitz/Corbis-Bettmann; p. 20 © Reuters/Andy Clark/Archive Photos.

Drohan, Michele Ingber.
    Learning about strength of character from the life of Muhammad Ali / by Michele Ingber Drohan.
       p.   cm. — (A character building book)
    Includes index.
    Summary: A brief biography of the champion boxer, Muhammad Ali, emphasizing how he demonstrated the courage of his convictions.
    ISBN 0-8239-5347-5
    1. Ali, Muhammad, 1942– —Juvenile literature. 2. Boxers (Sports)—United States—Biography—Juvenile literature. [1. Ali, Muhammad, 1942– . 2. Boxers (Sports). 3. Afro-Americans—Biography. 4. Self-confidence.] I. Title. II. Series.
GV1132.A44D76 1998
796.83'092—dc21
[B]
                                               98-26483
                                               CIP
                                               AC

Manufactured in the United States of America

Contents

Cassius Clay

On January 17, 1942, the greatest boxer of all time was born. His name was Cassius Marcellus Clay, Jr. He grew up in Louisville, Kentucky, which was **segregated** (SEH-grih-gay-ted) at that time. This meant that black people had to go to different schools, hospitals, restaurants, and churches than white people. This hurt all black people, including Cassius. But his parents always told him that if he had strength of **character** (KAR-ak-ter) he could be the best at whatever he did. He believed them.

◄ *Muhammad Ali is more than just a great fighter. He's made a difference in people's lives around the world.*

5

The Stolen Bicycle

Cassius Clay's life changed the day his bicycle was stolen. When twelve-year-old Cassius went to the police, he met officer Joe Martin. Cassius told him he wanted to find the person who had stolen his bike. Joe said that Cassius should first learn how to **defend** (dih-FEND) himself, in case the thief tried to fight him. Joe Martin wasn't only a policeman. He also taught boys how to box. He began teaching Cassius how to box. Cassius worked hard and grew stronger. Later he would become Joe's most famous student.

Cassius Clay started boxing when he was twelve. ▶
This is the first boxing photo taken of him.

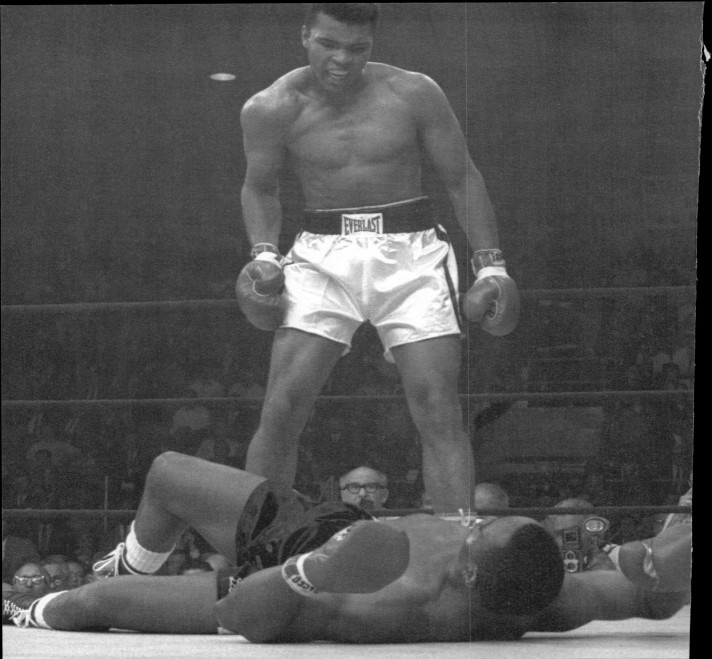

A New Name

Cassius became a great boxer. In 1964 he beat Sonny Liston to become the boxing **champion** (CHAM-pee-un) of the world. Then Cassius joined the **Nation of Islam** (NAY-shun of IZ-lam). He changed his name to Muhammad Ali. Many people were shocked because the Nation of Islam said that black people should be separate from white people. But Muhammad believed in himself and in the Nation of Islam. People didn't agree with Muhammad's choices, but they still respected him because he stood up for his beliefs.

◀ This is the last time Cassius Clay fought using his birth name. Nine days later he became Muhammad Ali.

Refusing to Fight

At the same time that Muhammad was champion, the United States was fighting a war in a country called Vietnam. Muhammad believed war was wrong. Because of his religion, he refused to join the army. The government took away his championship title and told him that he couldn't box anymore. Even though Muhammad **sacrificed** (SA-krih-fysd) all he had worked for in boxing, he knew it was the right thing to do. He spent this time speaking out against the Vietnam War and fighting for the rights of black Americans.

Even though he lost his title, Muhammad was proud of his decision not to fight in Vietnam. ▶

Poetry in Motion

During Muhammad's **exile** (EG-zyl), he became more and more popular. He was the most **recognized** (REH-kig-nyzd) face in the world. People loved him not only for his strength, but for his sense of humor. One of the things he became known for was his poetry. His most famous line talks about the way he moved in the ring: "Float Like a Butterfly, Sting Like a Bee!" He also wrote one of the shortest poems ever: "Me/Whee!" After spending four years outside the boxing ring, Muhammad was finally allowed to fight again.

◀ *Muhammad liked showing off to reporters and photographers. He would tell everyone, "I am The Greatest!"*

13

"Rumble in the Jungle"

Muhammad wanted to win back his championship title. He had to fight the champion George Foreman to do it. The fight took place in the African country of Zaire. Many people didn't believe Muhammad could win because George was bigger and hit harder. But Muhammad believed in himself and beat George. Muhammad became champion of the world again. Winning this fight was very important. For Muhammad, it meant that if you stand up for what you believe in, you will win in the end.

After the fight, Muhammad told his friends, "You'll never know how long I waited for this. You'll ▶ *never know what this means to me."*

A Turning Point

In 1975 Elijah Muhammad, the leader of the Nation of Islam, died. His son Wallace became the new leader. Wallace didn't believe that blacks should be separate from whites. He believed the true meaning of the Nation of Islam was to love all people, no matter what color they are. Some people in the Nation were upset by this change. But Muhammad agreed with Wallace and felt it was the right way to think. Since then Muhammad's beliefs have grown even stronger.

◄ *Elijah Muhammad was Muhammad's religious leader and friend. He gave Muhammad Ali his name.*

Parkinson's Syndrome

In 1984 Muhammad was **diagnosed** (DY-ug-nohst) with a disease called **Parkinson's syndrome** (PAR-kin-sinz SIN-drohm). This disease causes many physical problems, such as shaky hands and difficulty with speech. But even though his body has slowed down, his mind has not been affected. Muhammad doesn't let his disease stop him from spreading his message of love or helping those in need. And the love he gets from people around the world gives him the strength to keep going.

Doctors believe that Muhammad got Parkinson's syndrome from being in so many fights for so many years. ▶

The Olympic Torch

Muhammad was asked to carry the torch at the 1996 Olympic Games in Atlanta, Georgia. He would be the person to light the **cauldron** (KAWL-drun) that marks the start of the Olympics. This was a very special **honor** (ON-er) for him. In 1960 Muhammad won a gold medal in boxing at the Olympics in Rome. This time more than 3 billion people watched him light the cauldron. Muhammad showed them all once again that the strongest people are those who are strong on the inside.

◀ *Carrying the Olympic torch was a very special moment for Muhammad. Later he received a new gold medal to replace his old one, which he lost years ago.*

At Peace

Muhammad begins each day at 5:00 AM with a prayer. He spends lots of time with his family. Muhammad also travels to other countries to help solve problems. He's met with many world leaders and touched many lives. Once the greatest fighter in the world, he is now at peace with his illness and the person he has become. When people think of Muhammad, they say, "Ali had the strength of character to stand up for what he believed." And that's what he'll be remembered for.

Glossary

cauldron (KAWL-drun) A large kettle that holds the Olympic flame.

champion (CHAM-pee-un) The winner of first prize in a competition.

character (KAR-ak-ter) The way a person acts.

defend (dih-FEND) To protect yourself.

diagnose (DY-ug-nohs) To decide that a person has a condition or disease.

exile (EG-zyl) When you are forced out of something.

honor (ON-er) A privilege given to someone.

Nation of Islam (NAY-shun of IZ-lam) A religion started in the 1930s by Elijah Muhammad.

Parkinson's syndrome (PAR-kin-sinz SIN-drohm) A disease that causes shaking and difficulty speaking.

recognize (REH-kig-nyz) To know.

sacrifice (SA-krih-fys) To give up something for an ideal or belief.

segregate (SEH-grih-gayt) To separate people of different races.

Index